Marx Joyce Abbott Hardy Machiavelli Montaigne Chesterton Cooper Emerson Austen Defoe Melville Haggard Hugo Eliot Grimm Carroll Christie Stoker Molière Wilde Maupassant Byron Schiller Engels Garnett Einstein Fitzgerald Smith Hawthorne Kafka Goethe Dostoyevsky Hall Cotton Baum Kipling Doyle Willis Leslie Dumas Henry Nietzsche Flaubert Turgenev Balzac Stockton Vatsyayana Crane Burroughs Verne Curtis Tocqueville Whitman Gogol Vinci Homer Widger Tolstoy Busch Darwin Thoreau Scott Potter Freud Zola Twain Plato Lawrence Kant Jowett Stevenson Dickens Andersen Burton Hesse Harte London Descartes Cervantes Voltaire Poe Aristotle Wells Hale James Hastings Cooke Bunner Shakespeare Richter Chambers Irving Doré da Chekhov Shaw Wodehouse Benedict Alcott Swift Dante Pushkin Newton tredition®

tredition was established in 2006 by Sandra Latusseck and Soenke Schulz. Based in Hamburg, Germany, tredition offers publishing solutions to authors and publishing houses, combined with worldwide distribution of printed and digital book content. tredition is uniquely positioned to enable authors and publishing houses to create books on their own terms and without conventional manufacturing risks.

For more information please visit: www.tredition.com

TREDITION CLASSICS

This book is part of the TREDITION CLASSICS series. The creators of this series are united by passion for literature and driven by the intention of making all public domain books available in printed format again - worldwide. Most TREDITION CLASSICS titles have been out of print and off the bookstore shelves for decades. At tredition we believe that a great book never goes out of style and that its value is eternal. Several mostly non-profit literature projects provide content to tredition. To support their good work, tredition donates a portion of the proceeds from each sold copy. As a reader of a TREDITION CLASSICS book, you support our mission to save many of the amazing works of world literature from oblivion. See all available books at www.tredition.com.

Project Gutenberg

The content for this book has been graciously provided by Project Gutenberg. Project Gutenberg is a non-profit organization founded by Michael Hart in 1971 at the University of Illinois. The mission of Project Gutenberg is simple: To encourage the creation and distribution of eBooks. Project Gutenberg is the first and largest collection of public domain eBooks.

History of the United Netherlands, 1588d

John Lothrop Motley

Imprint

This book is part of TREDITION CLASSICS

Author: John Lothrop Motley
Cover design: Buchgut, Berlin – Germany

Publisher: tredition GmbH, Hamburg - Germany
ISBN: 978-3-8424-5723-2

www.tredition.com
www.tredition.de

CHAPTER XIX. Part 2.

And in Calais roads the great fleet—sailing slowly all next day in company with the English, without a shot being fired on either side—at last dropped anchor on Saturday afternoon, August 6th.

Here then the Invincible Armada had arrived at its appointed resting- place. Here the great junction—of Medina Sidonia with the Duke of Parma was to be effected; and now at last the curtain was to rise upon the last act of the great drama so slowly and elaborately prepared.

That Saturday afternoon, Lord Henry Seymour and his squadron of sixteen lay between Dungeness and Folkestone; waiting the approach of the two fleets. He spoke several-coasting vessels coming from the west; but they could give him no information—strange to say—either of the Spaniards or, of his own countrymen,—Seymour; having hardly three days' provision in his fleet, thought that there might be time to take in supplies; and so bore into the Downs. Hardly had he been there half an hour; when a pinnace arrived from the Lord-Admiral; with orders for Lord Henry's squadron to hold itself in readiness. There was no longer time for victualling, and very soon afterwards the order was given to make sail and bear for the French coast. The wind was however so light; that the whole day was spent before Seymour with his ships could cross the channel. At last, towards seven in the evening; he saw the great Spanish Armada, drawn up in a half-moon, and riding at anchor—the ships very near each other—a little to the eastward of Calais, and very near the shore. The English, under Howard Drake, Frobisher, and Hawkins, were slowly following, and—so soon as Lord Henry, arriving from the opposite shore; had made his junction with them—the whole combined fleet dropped anchor likewise very near Calais, and within one mile and a half of the Spaniards. That invincible force had at last almost reached its destination. It was now to receive the cooperation of the great Farnese, at the head of an army of veterans, disciplined on a hundred battle- fields, confident from countless victories, and arrayed, as they had been with ostentatious splendour, to follow the most brilliant general in Christendom on his triumphal march into the capital of England. The long-threatened invasion was no longer an idle figment of politicians, maliciously spread abroad to poison men's minds as to the intentions of a long-enduring but magnanimous, and on the whole friendly sovereign. The mask had been at last thrown down, and the mild accents of Philip's diplomatists and their English dupes, interchanging protocols so decorously month after month on the sands of Bourbourg, had been drowned by the peremptory voice of English and Spanish artillery, suddenly breaking in upon their placid conferences. It had now become supererogatory to ask for Alexander's word of honour whether he had, ever heard of Cardinal Allan's pamphlet, or whether his master contemplated hostilities against Queen Elizabeth.

Never, since England was England, had such a sight been seen as now revealed itself in those narrow straits between Dover and Calais. Along that long, low, sandy shore, and quite within the range of the Calais fortifications, one hundred and thirty Spanish ships—the greater number of them the largest and most heavily armed in the world lay face to face, and scarcely out of cannon-shot, with one hundred and fifty English sloops and frigates, the strongest and swiftest that the island could furnish, and commanded by men whose exploits had rung through the world.

Farther along the coast, invisible, but known to be performing a post perilous and vital service, was a squadron of Dutch vessels of all sizes, lining both the inner and outer edges of the sandbanks off the Flemish coasts, and swarming in all the estuaries and inlets of that intricate and dangerous cruising-ground between Dunkerk and Walcheren. Those fleets of Holland and Zeeland, numbering some one hundred and fifty galleons, sloops, and fly-boats, under Warmond, Nassau, Van der Does, de Moor, and Rosendael, lay patiently blockading every possible egress from Newport, or Gravelines; or Sluys, or Flushing, or Dunkerk, and longing to grapple with the Duke of Parma, so soon as his fleet of gunboats and hoys, packed with his Spanish and Italian veterans, should venture to set forth upon the sea for their long-prepared exploit.

It was a pompous spectacle, that midsummer night, upon those narrow seas. The moon, which was at the full, was rising calmly upon a scene of anxious expectation. Would she not be looking, by the morrow's night, upon a subjugated England, a re-enslaved Holland—upon the downfall of civil and religious liberty? Those ships of Spain, which lay there with their banners waving in the moonlight, discharging salvoes of anticipated triumph and filling the air with strains of insolent music; would they not, by daybreak, be moving straight to their purpose, bearing the conquerors of the world to the scene of their cherished hopes?

That English fleet, too, which rode there at anchor, so anxiously on the watch—would that swarm of, nimble, lightly-handled, but slender vessels,—which had held their own hitherto in hurried and desultory skirmishes—be able to cope with their great antagonist now that the moment had arrived for the death grapple? Would not Howard, Drake, Frobisher, Seymour, Winter, and Hawkins, be swept out of the straits at last, yielding an open passage to Medina, Oquendo, Recalde, and Farnese? Would those Hollanders and Zeelanders, cruising so vigilantly among their treacherous shallows, dare to maintain their post, now that the terrible 'Holofernese,' with his invincible legions, was resolved to come forth?

So soon as he had cast anchor, Howard despatched a pinnace to the Vanguard, with a message to Winter to come on board the flagship. When Sir William reached the Ark, it was already nine in the evening. He was anxiously consulted by the Lord-Admiral as to the course now to be taken. Hitherto the English had been teasing and perplexing an enemy, on the retreat, as it were, by the nature of his instructions. Although anxious to give battle, the Spaniard was forbidden to descend upon the coast until after his junction with Parma. So the English had played a comparatively easy game, hanging upon their enemy's skirts, maltreating him as they doubled about him, cannonading him from a distance, and slipping out of his reach at their pleasure. But he was now to be met face to face, and the fate of the two free commonwealths of the world was upon the issue of the struggle, which could no longer be deferred.

Winter, standing side by aide with the Lord-Admiral on the deck of the little Ark-Royal, gazed for the first time on those enormous galleons and galleys with which his companion, was already sufficiently familiar.

"Considering their hugeness," said he, "twill not be possible to remove them but by a device."

Then remembering, in a lucky moment, something that he had heard four years before of the fire ships sent by the Antwerpers against Parma's bridge—the inventor of which, the Italian Gianibelli, was at that very moment constructing fortifications on the Thames to assist the English against his old enemy Farnese—Winter suggested that some stratagem of the same kind should be attempted against the Invincible Armada. There was no time nor opportunity to prepare such submarine volcanoes as had been employed on that memorable occasion; but burning ships at least might be sent among the fleet. Some damage would doubtless be thus inflicted by the fire, and perhaps a panic, suggested by the memories of Antwerp and by the knowledge that the famous Mantuan wizard was then a resident of England, would be still more effective. In Winter's opinion, the Armada might at least be compelled to slip its cables, and be thrown into some confusion if the project were fairly carried out.

Howard approved of the device, and determined to hold, next morning, a council of war for arranging the details of its execution.

While the two sat in the cabin, conversing thus earnestly, there had well nigh been a serious misfortune. The ship, White Bear, of 1000 tons burthen, and three others of the English fleet, all tangled together, came drifting with the tide against the Ark. There were many yards carried away; much tackle spoiled, and for a time there was great danger; in the opinion of Winter, that some of the very best ships in the fleet would be crippled and quite destroyed on the eve of a general engagement. By alacrity and good handling, however, the ships were separated, and the ill-consequences of an accident—such as had already proved fatal to several Spanish vessels—were fortunately averted.

Next day, Sunday, 7th August, the two great fleets were still lying but a mile and a half apart, calmly gazing at each other, and rising and falling at their anchors as idly as if some vast summer regatta were the only purpose of that great assemblage of shipping. Nothing as yet was heard of Farnese. Thus far, at least, the Hollanders had held him at bay, and there was still breathing-time before the catastrophe. So Howard hung out his signal for council early in the morning, and very soon after Drake and Hawkins, Seymour, Winter, and the rest, were gravely consulting in his cabin.

It was decided that Winter's suggestion should be acted upon, and Sir Henry Palmer was immediately despatched in a pinnace to Dover, to bring off a number of old vessels fit to be fired, together with a supply of light wood, tar, rosin, sulphur, and other combustibles, most adapted to the purpose.' But as time wore away, it became obviously impossible for Palmer to return that night, and it was determined to make the most of what could be collected in the fleet itself. Otherwise it was to be feared that the opportunity might be for ever lost. Parma, crushing all opposition, might suddenly appear at any moment upon the channel; and the whole Spanish Armada, placing itself between him and his enemies, would engage the English and Dutch fleets, and cover his passage to Dover. It would then be too late to think of the burning ships.

On the other hand, upon the decks of the Armada, there was an impatience that night which increased every hour. The governor of Calais; M. de Gourdon, had sent his nephew on board the flag-ship of Medina Sidonia, with courteous salutations, professions of friendship, and bountiful refreshments. There was no fear—now that Mucio was for the time in the ascendency—that the schemes of Philip would be interfered with by France. The governor, had, however, sent serious warning of—the dangerous position in which the Armada had placed itself. He was quite right. Calais roads were no safe anchorage for huge vessels like those of Spain and Portugal; for the tides and cross-currents to which they were exposed were most treacherous. It was calm enough at the moment, but a westerly gale might, in a few hours, drive the whole fleet hopelessly among the sand-banks of the dangerous Flemish coast. Moreover, the Duke, although tolerably well furnished with charts and pilots for the English coast, was comparatively unprovided against the dangers which might beset him off Dunkerk, Newport, and Flushing. He had sent messengers, day after day, to Farnese, begging for assistance of various kinds, but, above all, imploring his instant presence on the field of action. It was the time and, place for Alexander to assume the chief command. The Armada was ready to make front against the English fleet on the left, while on the right, the Duke, thus protected, might proceed across the channel and take possession of England.

And the impatience of the soldiers and sailors on board the fleet was equal to that of their commanders. There was London almost before their eyes—a huge mass of treasure, richer and more accessible than those mines beyond the Atlantic which had so often rewarded Spanish chivalry with fabulous wealth. And there were men in those galleons who remembered the sack of Antwerp, eleven years before—men who could tell, from personal experience, how helpless was a great commercial city, when once in the clutch of disciplined brigands—men who, in that dread 'fury of Antwerp,' had enriched themselves in an hour with the accumulations of a merchant's life-time, and who had slain fathers and mothers, sons and daughters, brides and bridegrooms, before each others' eyes, until the number of inhabitants butchered in the blazing streets rose to many thousands; and the plunder from palaces and warehouses was counted by millions; before the sun had set on the 'great fury.' Those Spaniards, and Italians, and Walloons, were now thirsting for more gold, for more blood; and as the capital of England was even more wealthy and far more defenceless than the commercial metropolis of the Netherlands had been, so it was resolved that the London 'fury' should be more thorough and more productive than the 'fury' of Antwerp, at the memory—of which the world still shuddered. And these professional soldiers had been taught to consider the English as a pacific, delicate, effeminate race, dependent on good living, without experience of war, quickly fatigued and discouraged, and even more easily to be plundered and butchered than were the excellent burghers of Antwerp.

And so these southern conquerors looked down from their great galleons and galeasses upon the English vessels. More than three quarters of them were merchantmen. There was no comparison whatever between the relative strength of the fleets. In number they were about equal being each from one hundred and thirty to one hundred and fifty strong—but the Spaniards had twice the tonnage of the English, four times the artillery, and nearly three times the number of men.

Where was Farnese? Most impatiently the Golden Duke paced the deck of the Saint Martin. Most eagerly were thousands of eyes strained towards the eastern horizon to catch the first glimpse of Parma's flotilla. But the day wore on to its close, and still the same inexplicable and mysterious silence prevailed. There was utter solitude on the waters in the direction of Gravelines and Dunkerk—not a sail upon the sea in the quarter where bustle and activity had been most expected. The mystery was profound, for it had never entered the head of any man in the Armada that Alexander could not come out when he chose.

And now to impatience succeeded suspicion and indignation; and there were curses upon sluggishness and upon treachery. For in the horrible atmosphere of duplicity, in which all Spaniards and Italians of that epoch lived, every man: suspected his brother, and already Medina Sidonia suspected Farnese of playing him false. There were whispers of collusion between the Duke and the English commissioners at Bourbourg. There were hints that Alexander was playing his own game, that he meant to divide the sovereignty of the Netherlands with the heretic Elizabeth, to desert his great trust, and to effect, if possible, the destruction of his master's Armada, and the downfall of his master's sovereignty in the north. Men told each other, too, of a vague rumour, concerning which Alexander might have received information, and in which many believed, that Medina Sidonia was the bearer of secret orders to throw Farnese into bondage, so soon as he should appear, to send him a disgraced captive back to Spain for punishment, and to place the baton of command in the hand of the Duke of Pastrana, Philip's bastard by the Eboli. Thus, in the absence of Alexander, all was suspense and suspicion. It seemed possible that disaster instead of triumph was in store for them through the treachery of the commander-in-chief. Four and twenty hours and more, they had been lying in that dangerous roadstead, and although the weather had been calm and the sea tranquil, there seemed something brooding in the atmosphere.

As the twilight deepened, the moon became totally obscured, dark cloud- masses spread over the heavens, the sea grew black, distant thunder rolled, and the sob of an approaching tempest became distinctly audible. Such indications of a westerly gale, were not encouraging to those cumbrous vessels, with the treacherous quicksands of Flanders under their lee.

At an hour past midnight, it was so dark that it was difficult for the most practiced eye to pierce far into the gloom. But a faint drip of oars now struck the ears of the Spaniards as they watched from the decks. A few moments afterwards the sea became, suddenly luminous, and six flaming vessels appeared at a slight distance, bearing steadily down upon them before the wind and tide.

There were men in the Armada who had been at the siege of Antwerp only three years before. They remembered with horror the devil-ships of Gianibelli, those floating volcanoes, which had seemed to rend earth and ocean, whose explosion had laid so many thousands of soldiers dead at a blow, and which had shattered the bridge and floating forts of Farnese, as though they had been toys of glass. They knew, too, that the famous engineer was at that moment in England.

In a moment one of those horrible panics, which spread with such contagious rapidity among large bodies of men, seized upon the Spaniards. There was a yell throughout the fleet—"the fire-ships of Antwerp, the fire-ships of Antwerp!" and in an instant every cable was cut, and frantic attempts were made by each galleon and galeasse to escape what seemed imminent destruction. The confusion was beyond description. Four or five of the largest ships became entangled with each other. Two others were set on fire by the flaming—vessels, and were consumed. Medina Sidonia, who had been warned, even, before his departure from Spain, that some such artifice would probably be attempted, and who had even, early that morning, sent out a party of sailors in a pinnace to search for indications of the scheme, was not surprised or dismayed. He gave orders—as well as might be that every ship, after the danger should be passed, was to return to its post, and, await his further orders. But it was useless, in that moment of unreasonable panic to issue commands. The despised Mantuan, who had met with so many rebuffs at Philip's court, and who—owing to official incredulity had been but partially successful in his magnificent enterprise at Antwerp, had now; by the mere terror of his name, inflicted more damage on Philip's Armada than had hitherto been accomplished by Howard and Drake, Hawkins and Frobisher, combined.

So long as night and darkness lasted, the confusion and uproar continued. When the Monday morning dawned, several of the Spanish vessels lay disabled, while the rest of the fleet was seen at a distance of two leagues from Calais, driving towards the Flemish coast. The threatened gale had not yet begun to blow, but there were fresh squalls from the W.S.W., which, to such awkward sailers as the Spanish vessels; were difficult to contend with. On the other hand, the English fleet were all astir; and ready to pursue the Spaniards, now rapidly drifting into the North Sea. In the immediate neighbourhood of Calais, the flagship of the squadron of galeasses, commanded by Don Hugo de Moncada, was discovered using her foresail and oars, and endeavouring to enter the harbour. She had been damaged by collision with the St. John of Sicily and other ships, during the night's panic, and had her rudder quite torn away. She was the largest and most splendid vessel in the Armada—the show-ship of the fleet,—"the very glory and stay of the Spanish navy," and during the previous two days she had been visited and admired by great numbers of Frenchmen from the shore.

Lord Admiral Howard bore dawn upon her at once, but as she was already in shallow water, and was rowing steadily towards the town, he saw that the Ark could not follow with safety. So he sent his long-boat to cut her out, manned with fifty or sixty volunteers, most of them "as valiant in courage as gentle in birth"—as a partaker in the adventure declared. The Margaret and Joan of London, also following in pursuit, ran herself aground, but the master despatched his pinnace with a body of musketeers, to aid in the capture of the galeasse.

That huge vessel failed to enter the harbour, and stuck fast upon the bar. There was much dismay on board, but Don Hugo prepared resolutely to defend himself. The quays of Calais and the line of the French shore were lined with thousands of eager spectators, as the two boats-rowing steadily toward a galeasse, which carried forty brass pieces of artillery, and was manned with three hundred soldiers and four hundred and fifty slaves—seemed rushing upon their own destruction. Of these daring Englishmen, patricians and plebeians together, in two open pinnaces, there were not more than one hundred in number, all told. They soon laid themselves close to the Capitana, far below her lofty sides, and called on Don Hugo to surrender. The answer was, a smile of derision from the haughty Spaniard, as he looked down upon them from what seemed an inaccessible height. Then one Wilton, coxswain of the Delight; of Winter's squadron, clambered up to the enemy's deck and fell dead the same instant. Then the English volunteers opened a volley upon the Spaniards; "They seemed safely ensconced in their ships," said bold Dick Tomson, of the Margaret and Joan, "while we in our open pinnaces, and far under them, had nothing to shroud and cover us." Moreover the numbers were, seven hundred and fifty to one hundred. But, the Spaniards, still quite disconcerted by the events of the preceding night, seemed under a spell. Otherwise it would have been an easy matter for the great galeasse to annihilate such puny antagonists in a very short space of time.

The English pelted the Spaniards quite cheerfully, however, with arquebus shot, whenever they showed themselves above the bulwarks, picked off a considerable number, and sustained a rather severe loss themselves, Lieutenant Preston of the Ark-Royal, among others, being dangerously wounded. "We had a pretty skirmish for half-an-hour," said Tomson. At last Don Hugo de Moncada, furious at the inefficiency of his men, and leading them forward in person, fell back on his deck with a bullet through both eyes. The panic was instantaneous, for, meantime, several other English boats—some with eight, ten; or twelve men on board—were seen pulling—towards the galeasse; while the dismayed soldiers at once leaped overboard on the land side, and attempted to escape by swimming and wading to the shore. Some of them succeeded, but the greater number were drowned. The few who remained—not more, than twenty in all— hoisted two handkerchiefs upon two rapiers as a signal of truce. The English, accepting it as a signal of defeat; scrambled with great difficulty up the lofty sides of the Capitana, and, for an hour and a half, occupied themselves most agreeably in plundering the ship and in liberating the slaves.

It was their intention, with the flood-tide, to get the vessel off, as she was but slightly damaged, and of very great value. But a serious obstacle arose to this arrangement. For presently a boat came along-side, with young M. de Gourdon and another French captain, and hailed the galeasse. There was nobody on board who could speak French but Richard Tomson. So Richard returned the hail, and asked their business. They said they came from the governor.

"And what is the—governor's pleasure?" asked Tomson, when they had come up the side.

"The governor has stood and beheld your fight, and rejoiced in your victory," was the reply; "and he says that for your prowess and manhood you well deserve the pillage of the galeasse. He requires and commands you, however, not to attempt carrying off either the ship or its ordnance; for she lies a-ground under the battery of his castle, and within his jurisdiction, and does of right appertain to him."

This seemed hard upon the hundred volunteers, who, in their two open boats, had so manfully carried a ship of 1200 tons, 40 guns, and 750 men; but Richard answered diplomatically.

"We thank M. de Gourdon," said he, "for granting the pillage to mariners and soldiers who had fought for it, and we acknowledge that without his good-will we cannot carry away anything we have got, for the ship lies on ground directly under his batteries and bulwarks. Concerning the ship and ordnance, we pray that he would send a pinnace to my Lord Admiral Howard, who is here in person hard by, from whom he will have an honourable and friendly answer, which we shall all-obey."

With this—the French officers, being apparently content, were about to depart, and it is not impossible that the soft answer might have obtained the galeasse and the ordnance, notwithstanding the arrangement which Philip II. had made with his excellent friend Henry III. for aid and comfort to Spanish vessels in French ports. Unluckily, however, the inclination for plunder being rife that morning, some of the Englishmen hustled their French visitors, plundered them of their rings and jewels, as if they had been enemies, and then permitted them to depart. They rowed off to the shore, vowing vengeance, and within a few minutes after their return the battery of the fort was opened upon the English, and they were compelled to make their escape as they could with the plunder already secured, leaving the galeasse in the possession of M. de Gourdon.

This adventure being terminated, and the pinnaces having returned to the fleet, the Lord-Admiral, who had been lying off and on, now bore away with all his force in pursuit of the Spaniards. The Invincible Armada, already sorely crippled, was standing N.N.E. directly before a fresh topsail-breeze from the S.S.W. The English came up with them soon after nine o'clock A.M. off Gravelines, and found them sailing in a half-moon, the admiral and vice-admiral in the centre, and the flanks protected by the three remaining galeasses and by the great galleons of Portugal.

Seeing the enemy approaching, Medina Sidonia ordered his whole fleet to luff to the wind, and prepare for action. The wind shifting a few points, was now at W.N.W., so that the English had both the weather-gage and the tide in their favour. A general combat began at about ten, and it was soon obvious to the Spaniards that their adversaries were intending warm work. Sir Francis Drake in the Revenge, followed by, Frobisher in the Triumph, Hawkins in the Victory, and some smaller vessels, made the first attack upon the Spanish flagships. Lord Henry in the Rainbow, Sir Henry Palmer in the Antelope, and others, engaged with three of the largest galleons of the Armada, while Sir William Winter in the Vanguard, supported by most of his squadron, charged the starboard wing.

The portion of the fleet thus assaulted fell back into the main body. Four of the ships ran foul of each other, and Winter, driving into their centre, found himself within musket-shot of many of their most formidable' ships.

"I tell you, on the credit of a poor gentleman," he said, "that there were five hundred discharges of demi-cannon, culverin, and demi-culverin, from the Vanguard; and when I was farthest off in firing my pieces, I was not out of shot of their harquebus, and most time within speech, one of another."

The battle lasted six hours long, hot and furious; for now there was no excuse for retreat on the part of the Spaniards, but, on the contrary, it was the intention of the Captain-General to return to his station off Calais, if it were within his power. Nevertheless the English still partially maintained the tactics which had proved so successful, and resolutely refused the fierce attempts of the Spaniards to lay themselves along-side. Keeping within musket-range, the well-disciplined English mariners poured broadside after broadside against the towering ships of the Armada, which afforded so easy a mark; while the Spaniards, on their part, found it impossible, while wasting incredible quantities of powder and shot, to inflict any severe damage on their enemies. Throughout the action, not an English ship was destroyed, and not a hundred men were killed. On the other hand, all the best ships of the Spaniards were riddled through and through, and with masts and yards shattered, sails and rigging torn to shreds, and a north-went wind still drifting them towards the fatal sand-batiks of Holland, they, laboured heavily in a chopping sea, firing wildly, and receiving tremendous punishment at the hands of Howard Drake, Seymour, Winter, and their followers. Not even master-gunner Thomas could complain that day of "blind exercise" on the part of the English, with "little harm done" to the enemy. There was scarcely a ship in the Armada that did not suffer severely, for nearly all were engaged in that memorable action off the sands of Gravelines. The Captain-General himself, Admiral Recalde, Alonzo de Leyva, Oquendo, Diego Flores de Valdez, Bertendona, Don Francisco de Toledo, Don Diego de Pimentel, Telles Enriquez, Alonzo de Luzon, Garibay, with most of the great galleons and galeasses, were in the thickest of the fight, and one after the other each of those huge ships was disabled. Three sank before the fight was over, many others were soon drifting helpless wrecks towards a hostile shore, and, before five o'clock, in the afternoon, at least sixteen of their best ships had been sacrificed, and from four to five thousand soldiers killed.

> ["God hath mightily preserved her Majesty's forces with the least losses that ever hath been heard of, being within the compass of so great volleys of shot, both small and great. I verily believe there is not threescore men lost of her Majesty's forces." Captain J. Fenner to Walsingham, 4/14 Aug. 1588. (S. P. Office MS.)]

Nearly all the largest vessels of the Armada, therefore, having, been disabled or damaged—according to a Spanish eye-witness—and all their small shot exhausted, Medina Sidonia reluctantly gave orders to retreat. The Captain-General was a bad sailor; but he was, a chivalrous Spaniard of ancient Gothic blood, and he felt deep mortification at the plight of his invincible fleet, together with undisguised: resentment against Alexander Farnese, through whose treachery and incapacity, he considered. the great Catholic cause to have been, so foully sacrificed. Crippled, maltreated, and diminished in number, as were his ships; he would have still faced, the enemy, but the winds and currents were fast driving him on, a lee-shore, and the pilots, one and all, assured him that it would be inevitable destruction to remain. After a slight and very ineffectual attempt to rescue Don Diego de Pimentel in the St. Matthew—who refused to leave his disabled ship—and Don Francisco de Toledo; whose great galleon, the St. Philip, was fast driving, a helpless wreck, towards Zeeland, the Armada bore away N.N.E. into the open sea, leaving those, who could not follow, to their fate.

The St. Matthew, in a sinking condition, hailed a Dutch fisherman, who was offered a gold chain to pilot her into Newport. But the fisherman, being a patriot; steered her close to the Holland fleet, where she was immediately assaulted by Admiral Van der Does, to whom, after a two hours' bloody fight, she struck her flag. Don Diego, marshal of the camp to the famous legion of Sicily, brother, of the Marquis of Tavera, nephew of the Viceroy of Sicily, uncle to the Viceroy of Naples, and numbering as many titles, dignities; and high affinities as could be expected of a grandee of the first class, was taken, with his officers, to the Hague. "I was the means," said Captain Borlase, "that the best sort were saved, and the rest were cast overboard and slain at our entry. He, fought with us two hours; and hurt divers of our men, but at, last yielded."

John Van der Does, his captor; presented the banner; of the Saint Matthew to the great church of Leyden, where—such was its prodigious length—it hung; from floor to ceiling without being entirely unrolled; and there hung, from generation to generation; a worthy companion to the Spanish flags which had been left behind when Valdez abandoned the siege of that heroic city fifteen years before.

The galleon St. Philip, one of the four largest ships in the Armada, dismasted and foundering; drifted towards Newport, where camp-marshal Don Francisco de Toledo hoped in, vain for succour. La

Motte made a feeble attempt at rescue, but some vessels from the Holland fleet, being much more active, seized the unfortunate galleon, and carried her into Flushing. The captors found forty-eight brass cannon and other things of value on board, but there were some casks of Ribadavia wine which was more fatal to her enemies than those pieces of artillery had proved. For while the rebels were refreshing themselves, after the fatigues of the capture, with large draughts of that famous vintage, the St. Philip, which had been bored through and through with English shot, and had been rapidly filling with water, gave a sudden lurch, and went down in a moment, carrying with her to the bottom three hundred of those convivial Hollanders.

A large Biscay galleon, too, of Recalde's squadron, much disabled in action, and now, like many others, unable to follow the Armada, was summoned by Captain Cross of the Hope, 48 guns, to surrender. Although foundering, she resisted, and refused to strike her flag. One of her officers attempted to haul down her colours, and was run through the body by the captain, who, in his turn, was struck dead by a brother of the officer thus slain. In the midst of this quarrel the ship went down with all her crew.

Six hours and more, from ten till nearly five, the fight had lasted— a most cruel battle, as the Spaniard declared. There were men in the Armada who had served in the action of Lepanto, and who declared that famous encounter to have been far surpassed in severity and spirit by this fight off Gravelines. "Surely every man in our fleet did well," said Winter, "and the slaughter the enemy received was great." Nor would the Spaniards have escaped even worse punishment, had not, most unfortunately, the penurious policy of the Queen's government rendered her ships useless at last, even in this supreme moment. They never ceased cannonading the discomfited enemy until the ammunition was exhausted. "When the cartridges were all spent," said Winter, "and the munitions in some vessels gone altogether, we ceased fighting, but followed the enemy, who still kept away." And the enemy—although still numerous, and seeming strong enough, if properly handled, to destroy the whole English fleet—fled before them. There remained more than fifty Spanish vessels, above six hundred tons in size, besides sixty hulks and other vessels of less account; while in the whole English navy were but thirteen ships of or above that burthen. "Their force is wonderful great and strong," said Howard, "but we pluck their feathers by little and little."

For Medina Sidonia had now satisfied himself that he should never succeed in boarding those hard-fighting and swift-sailing craft, while, meantime, the horrible panic of Sunday night and the succession of fights throughout the following day, had completely disorganized his followers. Crippled, riddled, shorn, but still numerous, and by no means entirely vanquished, the Armada was flying with a gentle breeze before an enemy who, to save his existence; could not have fired a broadside.

"Though our powder and shot was well nigh spent," said the Lord-Admiral, "we put on a brag countenance and gave them chase, as though we had wanted nothing." And the brag countenance was successful, for that "one day's service had much appalled the enemy" as Drake observed; and still the Spaniards fled with a freshening gale all through the Monday night. "A thing greatly to be regarded," said Fenner, of the Nonpariel, "is that that the Almighty had stricken them with a wonderful fear. I have hardly, seen any of their companies succoured of the extremities which befell them after their fights, but they have been left, at utter ruin, while they bear as much sail as ever they possibly can."

On Tuesday morning, 9th August, the English ships were off the isle of Walcheren, at a safe distance from the shore. "The wind is hanging westerly," said Richard Tomson, of the Margaret and Joan, "and we drive our enemies apace, much marvelling in what port they will direct themselves. Those that are left alive are so weak and heartless that they could be well content to lose all charges and to be at home, both rich and poor."

"In my, conscience," said Sir William Winter, "I think the Duke would give his dukedom to be in Spain again."

The English ships, one-hundred and four in number, being that morning half-a-league to windward, the Duke gave orders for the whole Armada to lay to and, await their approach. But the English had no disposition to engage, for at, that moment the instantaneous destruction of their enemies seemed inevitable. Ill-managed, panic-struck, staggering before their foes, the Spanish fleet was now close upon the fatal sands of Zeeland. Already there were but six and a-half fathoms of water, rapidly shoaling under their keels, and the pilots told Medina that all were irretrievably lost, for the freshening north-welter was driving them steadily upon the banks. The English, easily escaping the danger, hauled their wind, and paused to see the ruin of the proud Armada accomplished before their eyes. Nothing but a change of wind at the instant could save them from perdition. There was a breathless shudder of suspense, and then there came the change. Just as the foremost ships were about to ground on the Ooster Zand, the wind suddenly veered to the south-west, and the Spanish ships quickly squaring their sails to the new impulse, stood out once more into the open sea.

All that day the galleons and galeasses, under all the canvas which they dared to spread, continued their flight before the south-westerly breeze, and still the Lord-Admiral, maintaining the brag countenance, followed, at an easy distance, the retreating foe. At 4 p. m., Howard fired a signal gun, and ran up a flag of council. Winter could not go, for he had been wounded in action, but Seymour and Drake, Hawkins, Frobisher, and the rest were present, and it was decided that Lord Henry should return, accompanied by Winter and the rest of the inner, squadron, to guard the Thames mouth against any attempt of the Duke of Parma, while the Lord Admiral and the rest of the navy should continue the pursuit of the Armada.

Very wroth was Lord Henry at being deprived of his share in the chase. "The Lord-Admiral was altogether desirous to have me strengthen him," said he, "and having done so to the utmost of my good-will and the venture of my life, and to the distressing of the Spaniards, which was thoroughly done on the Monday last, I now find his Lordship jealous and loath to take part of the honour which is to come. So he has used his authority to command me to look to our English coast, threatened by the Duke of Parma. I pray God my Lord Admiral do not find the lack of the Rainbow and her companions, for I protest before God I vowed I would be as near or nearer with my little ship to encounter our enemies as any of the greatest ships in both armies."

There was no insubordination, however, and Seymour's squadron; at twilight of Tuesday evening, August 9th—according to orders, so that the enemy might not see their departure—bore away for Margate. But although Winter and Seymour were much disappointed at their enforced return, there was less enthusiasm among the sailors of the fleet. Pursuing the Spaniards without powder or fire, and without beef and bread to eat, was not thought amusing by the English crews. Howard had not three days' supply of food in his lockers, and Seymour and his squadron had not food for one day. Accordingly, when Seymour and Winter took their departure, "they had much ado," so Winter said; "with the staying of many ships that would have returned with them, besides their own company." Had the Spaniards; instead of being panic-struck, but turned on their pursuers, what might have been the result of a conflict with starving and unarmed men?

Howard, Drake, and Frobisher, with the rest of the fleet, followed the Armada through the North Sea from Tuesday night (9th August) till Friday (the 12th), and still, the strong southwester swept the Spaniards before them, uncertain whether to seek refuge, food, water, and room to repair damages, in the realms of the treacherous King of Scots, or on the iron- bound coasts of Norway. Medina Sidonia had however quite abandoned his intention of returning to England, and was only anxious for a safe return: to Spain. So much did he dread that northern passage; unpiloted, around the grim Hebrides, that he would probably have surrendered, had the English overtaken him and once more offered battle. He was on the point of hanging out a white flag as they approached him for the last time—but yielded to the expostulations of the ecclesiastics on board the Saint Martin, who thought, no doubt, that they had more to fear from England than from the sea, should they be carried captive to that country, and who persuaded him that it would be a sin and a disgrace to surrender before they had been once more attacked.

On the other hand, the Devonshire skipper, Vice-Admiral Drake, now thoroughly in his element, could not restrain his hilarity, as he saw the Invincible Armada of the man whose beard he had so often singed, rolling through the German Ocean, in full flight from the country which was to have been made, that week, a Spanish province. Unprovided as were his ships, he was for risking another battle, and it is quite possible that the brag countenance might have proved even more successful than Howard thought.

"We have the army of Spain before us," wrote Drake, from the Revenge, "and hope with the grace of God to wrestle a pull with him. There never was any thing pleased me better than seeing the enemy flying with a southerly wind to the northward. God grant you have a good eye to the Duke of Parma, for with the grace of God, if we live, I doubt not so to handle the matter with the Duke of Sidonia as he shall wish himself at St. Mary's Port among his orange trees."

But Howard decided to wrestle no further pull. Having followed the Spaniards till Friday, 12th of August, as far as the latitude of 56d. 17' the Lord Admiral called a council. It was then decided, in order to save English lives and ships, to put into the Firth of Forth for water and provisions, leaving two "pinnaces to dog, the fleet until it should be past the Isles of Scotland." But the next day, as the wind shifted to the north-west, another council decided to take advantage of the change, and bear away for the North Foreland, in order to obtain a supply of powder, shot, and provisions.

Up to this period, the weather, though occasionally threatening, had been moderate. During the week which succeeded the eventful night off. Calais, neither the 'Armada nor the English ships had been much impeded in their manoeuvres by storms of heavy seas. But on the following Sunday, 14th of August, there was a change. The wind shifted again to the south-west, and, during the whole of that day and the Monday, blew a tremendous gale. "'Twas a more violent storm," said Howard, "than was ever seen before at this time of the year." The retreating English fleet was, scattered, many ships were in peril, "among the ill-favoured sands off Norfolk," but within four or five days all arrived safely in Margate roads.

Far different was the fate of the Spaniards. Over their Invincible Armada, last seen by the departing English midway between the coasts of Scotland and Denmark, the blackness of night seemed suddenly to descend. A mystery hung for a long time over their fate. Damaged, leaking, without pilots, without a competent commander, the great fleet entered that furious storm, and was whirled along the iron crags of Norway and between the savage rocks of

Faroe and the Hebrides. In those regions of tempest the insulted North wreaked its full vengeance on the insolent Spaniards. Disaster after disaster marked their perilous track; gale after gale swept them hither and thither, tossing them on sandbanks or shattering them against granite cliffs. The coasts of Norway, Scotland, Ireland, were strewn with the wrecks of that pompous fleet, which claimed the dominion of the seas with the bones of those invincible legions which were to have sacked London and made England a Spanish vice-royalty.

Through the remainder of the month of August there, was a succession of storms. On the 2nd September a fierce southwester drove Admiral Oquendo in his galleon, together with one of the great galeasses, two large Venetian ships, the Ratty and the Balauzara, and thirty-six other vessels, upon the Irish coast, where nearly every soul on board perished, while the few who escaped to the shore—notwithstanding their religious affinity with the inhabitants—were either butchered in cold blood, or sent coupled in halters from village to village, in order to be shipped to England. A few ships were driven on the English coast; others went ashore near Rochelle.

Of the four galeasses and four galleys, one of each returned to Spain. Of the ninety-one great galleons and hulks, fifty-eight were lost and thirty-three returned. Of the tenders and zabras, seventeen were lost. and eighteen returned. Of one hundred and, thirty-four vessels, which sailed from Corona in July, but fifty-three, great and small, made their escape to Spain, and these were so damaged as to be, utterly worthless. The invincible Armada had not only been vanquished but annihilated.

Of the 30,000 men who sailed in the fleet; it is probable that not more than 10,000 ever saw their native land again. Most of the leaders of the expedition lost their lives. Medina Sidonia reached Santander in October, and, as Philip for a moment believed, "with the greater part of the Armada," although the King soon discovered his mistake. Recalde, Diego Flores de Valdez, Oquendo, Maldonado, Bobadilla, Manriquez, either perished at sea, or died of exhaustion immediately after their return. Pedro de Valdez, Vasco de Silva, Alonzo de Sayas, Piemontel, Toledo, with many other nobles, were prisoners in England and Holland. There was hardly a distinguished family in Spain not placed in mourning, so that, to relieve the universal gloom, an edict was published, forbidding the wearing of mourning at all. On the other hand, a merchant of Lisbon, not yet reconciled to the Spanish conquest of his country, permitted himself some tokens of hilarity at the defeat of the Armada, and was immediately hanged by express command of Philip. Thus—as men said—one could neither cry nor laugh within the Spanish dominions.

This was the result of the invasion, so many years preparing, and at an expense almost incalculable. In the year 1588 alone, the cost of Philip's armaments for the subjugation of England could not have been less than six millions of ducats, and there was at least as large a sum on board the Armada itself, although the Pope refused to pay his promised million. And with all this outlay, and with the sacrifice of so many thousand lives, nothing had been accomplished, and Spain, in a moment, instead of seeming terrible to all the world, had become ridiculous.

"Beaten and shuffled together from the Lizard to Calais, from Calais driven with squibs from their anchors, and chased out of sight of England about Scotland and Ireland," as the Devonshire skipper expressed himself, it must be confessed that the Spaniards presented a sorry sight. "Their invincible and dreadful navy," said Drake, "with all its great and terrible ostentation, did not in all their sailing about England so much as sink or take one ship, bark, pinnace, or cock-boat of ours, or even burn so much as one sheep-tote on this land."

Meanwhile Farnese sat chafing under the unjust reproaches heaped upon him, as if he, and not his master, had been responsible for the gigantic blunders of the invasion.

"As for the Prince of Parma," said Drake, "I take him to be as a bear robbed of her whelps." The Admiral was quite right. Alexander was beside himself with rage. Day after day, he had been repeating to Medina Sidonia and to Philip that his flotilla and transports could scarcely live in any but the smoothest sea, while the supposition that they could serve a warlike purpose he pronounced absolutely ludicrous. He had always counselled the seizing of a place like Flushing, as a basis of operations against England, but had been overruled; and he had at least reckoned upon the Invincible Armada to clear the way for him, before he should be expected to take the sea.

With prodigious energy and at great expense he had constructed or improved internal water-communications from Ghent to Sluy's, Newport, and Dunkerk. He had, thus transported all his hoys, barges, and munitions for the invasion, from all points of the obedient Netherlands to the sea- coast, without coming within reach of the Hollanders and Zeelanders, who were keeping close watch on the outside. But those Hollanders and Zeelanders, guarding every outlet to the ocean, occupying every hole and cranny of the coast, laughed the invaders of England to scorn, braving them, jeering them, daring them to come forth, while the Walloons and Spaniards shrank before such amphibious assailants, to whom a combat on the water was as natural as upon dry land. Alexander, upon one occasion, transported with rage, selected a band of one thousand musketeers, partly Spanish, partly Irish, and ordered an assault upon those insolent boatmen. With his own hand—so it was related—he struck dead more than one of his own officers who remonstrated against these commands; and then the attack was made by his thousand musketeers upon the Hollanders, and every man of the thousand was slain.

He had been reproached for not being ready, for not having embarked his men; but he had been ready for a month, and his men could be embarked in a single day. "But it was impossible," he said, "to keep them long packed up on board vessels, so small that there was no room to turn about in the people would sicken, would rot, would die." So soon as he had received information of the arrival of the fleet before Calais—which was on the 8th August—he had proceeded the same night to Newport and embarked 16,000 men, and before dawn he was at Dunkerk, where the troops stationed in that port were as rapidly placed on board the transports. Sir William Stanley, with his 700 Irish kernes, were among the first shipped for the enterprise. Two-days long these regiments lay heaped. together, like sacks of corn, in the boats—as one of their officers described it—and they lay cheerfully hoping that the Dutch fleet would be swept out of the sea by the Invincible Armada, and patiently expecting the signal for setting sail to England. Then came the Prince of

Ascoli, who had gone ashore from the Spanish fleet at Calais, accompanied by serjeant-major Gallinato and other messengers from Medina Sidonia, bringing the news of the fire-ships and the dispersion and flight of the Armada.

"God knows," said Alexander, "the distress in which this event has plunged me, at the very moment when I expected to be sending your Majesty my congratulations on the success of the great undertaking. But these are the works of the Lord, who can recompense your Majesty by giving you many victories, and the fulfilment of your Majesty's desires, when He thinks the proper time arrived. Meantime let Him be praised for all, and let your Majesty take great care of your health, which is the most important thing of all."

Evidently the Lord did not think the proper time yet arrived for fulfilling his Majesty's desires for the subjugation of England, and meanwhile the King might find what comfort he could in pious commonplaces and in attention to his health.

But it is very certain that, of all the high parties concerned, Alexander Farnese was the least reprehensible for the over-throw of Philips hopes. No man could have been more judicious—as it has been sufficiently made evident in the course of this narrative—in arranging all the details of the great enterprise, in pointing out all the obstacles, in providing for all emergencies. No man could have been more minutely faithful to his master, more treacherous to all the world beside. Energetic, inventive, patient, courageous; and stupendously false, he had covered Flanders with canals and bridges, had constructed flotillas, and equipped a splendid army, as thoroughly as he had puzzled Comptroller Croft. And not only had that diplomatist and his wiser colleagues been hoodwinked, but Elizabeth and Burghley, and, for a moment, even Walsingham, were in the, dark, while Henry III. had been his passive victim, and the magnificent Balafre a blind instrument in his hands. Nothing could equal Alexander's fidelity, but his perfidy. Nothing could surpass his ability to command but his obedience. And it is very possible that had Philip followed his nephew's large designs, instead of imposing upon him his own most puerile schemes; the result far England, Holland, and, all Christendom might have been very different from the actual one. The blunder against which Farnese had in vain warned his master, was the stolid ignorance in which the King and all his counsellors chose to remain of the Holland and Zeeland fleet. For them Warmond and Nassau, and Van der Does and Joost de Moor; did not exist, and it was precisely these gallant sailors, with their intrepid crews, who held the key to the whole situation.

To the Queen's glorious naval-commanders, to the dauntless mariners of England, with their well-handled vessels; their admirable seamanship, their tact and their courage, belonged the joys of the contest, the triumph, and the glorious pursuit; but to the patient Hollanders and Zeelanders, who, with their hundred vessels held Farneae, the chief of the great enterprise, at bay, a close prisoner with his whole army in his own ports, daring him to the issue, and ready—to the last plank of their fleet and to the last drop of their blood—to confront both him and the Duke of Medina Sidona, an equal share of honour is due. The safety of the two free commonwealths of the world in that terrible contest was achieved by the people and the mariners of the two states combined.

Great was the enthusiasm certainly of the English people as the volunteers marched through London to the place of rendezvous, and tremendous were the cheers when the brave Queen rode on horseback along the lines of Tilbury. Glowing pictures are revealed to us of merry little England, arising in its strength, and dancing forth to encounter the Spaniards, as if to a great holiday. "It was a pleasant sight," says that enthusiastic merchant-tailor John Stowe, "to behold the cheerful countenances, courageous words, and gestures, of the soldiers, as they marched to Tilbury, dancing, leaping wherever they came, as joyful at the news of the foe's approach as if lusty giants were to run a race. And Bellona-like did the Queen infuse a second spirit of loyalty, love, and resolution, into every soldier of her army, who, ravished with their sovereign's sight, prayed heartily that the Spaniards might land quickly, and when they heard they were fled, began to lament."

But if the Spaniards had not fled, if there had been no English navy in the Channel, no squibs at Calais, no Dutchmen off Dunkerk, there might have been a different picture to paint. No man who has, studied the history of those times, can doubt the universal and enthusiastic determination of the English nation to repel the invaders.

Catholics and Protestants felt alike on the great subject. Philip did not flatter, himself with assistance from any English Papists, save exiles and renegades like Westmoreland, Paget, Throgmorton, Morgan, Stanley, and the rest. The bulk of the Catholics, who may have constituted half the population of England, although malcontent, were not rebellious; and notwithstanding the precautionary measures taken by government against them, Elizabeth proudly acknowledged their loyalty.

But loyalty, courage, and enthusiasm, might not have sufficed to supply the want of numbers and discipline. According to the generally accepted statement of contemporary chroniclers, there were some 75,000 men under arms: 20,000 along the southern coast, 23,000 under Leicester, and 33,000 under Lord Chamberlain Hunsdon, for the special defence of the Queen's person.

But it would have been very difficult, in the moment of danger, to bring anything like these numbers into the field. A drilled and disciplined army—whether of regulars or of militia-men—had no existence whatever. If the merchant vessels, which had been joined to the royal fleet, were thought by old naval commanders to be only good to make a show, the volunteers on land were likely to be even less effective than the marine militia, so much more accustomed than they to hard work. Magnificent was the spirit of the great feudal lords as they rallied round their Queen. The Earl of Pembroke offered to serve at the head of three hundred horse and five hundred footmen, armed at his own cost, and all ready to "hazard the blood of their hearts" in defence of her person. "Accept hereof most excellent sovereign," said the Earl, "from a person desirous to live no longer than he may see your Highness enjoy your blessed estate, maugre the beards of all confederated leaguers."

The Earl of Shrewsbury, too, was ready to serve at the head of his retainers, to the last drop of his blood. "Though I be old," he said, "yet shall your quarrel make me young again. Though lame in body, yet lusty in heart to lend your greatest enemy one blow, and to stand near your defence, every way wherein your Highness shall employ me."

But there was perhaps too much of this feudal spirit. The lieutenant- general complained bitterly that there was a most mischievous tendency among all the militia-men to escape from the Queen's colours, in order to enrol themselves as retainers to the great lords. This spirit was not favourable to efficient organization of a national army. Even, had the commander-in-chief been a man, of genius and experience it would have been difficult for him, under such circumstances, to resist a splendid army, once landed, and led by Alexander Farnese, but even Leicester's most determined flatterers hardly ventured to compare him in-military ability with that first general of his age. The best soldier in England was un-questionably Sir John Norris, and Sir John was now marshal of the camp to Leicester. The ancient quarrel between the two had been smoothed over, and—as might be expected—the Earl hated Norris more bitterly than before, and was perpetually vituperating him, as he had often done in the Netherlands. Roger William, too, was entrusted with the important duties of master of the horse, under the lieutenant-general, and Leicester continued to bear the grudge towards that honest Welshman, which had begun in Holland. These were not promising conditions in a camp, when an invading army was every day expected; nor was the completeness or readiness of the forces sufficient to render harmless the quarrels of the commanders.

The Armada had arrived in Calais roads on Saturday afternoon; the 6th August. If it had been joined on that day, or the next—as Philip and Medina Sidonia fully expected—by the Duke of Parma's flotilla, the invasion would have been made at once. If a Spanish army had ever landed in England at all, that event would have occurred on the 7th August. The weather was not unfavourable; the sea was smooth, and the circumstances under which the catastrophe of the great drama was that night accomplished, were a profound mystery to every soul in England. For aught that Leicester, or Burghley, or Queen Elizabeth, knew at the time, the army of Farnese might, on Monday, have been marching upon London. Now, on that Monday morning, the army of Lord Hunsdon was not assembled at all, and Leicester with but four thousand men, under his command, was just commencing his camp at Tilbury. The. "Bellona-like" appearance of the Queen on her white palfrey,—with truncheon in hand, addressing her troops, in that magnificent burst of eloquence which has so often been repeated, was not till eleven days afterwards; not till the great Armada, shattered and tempest-tossed, had been, a week long, dashing itself against the cliffs of Norway and the Faroes, on, its forlorn retreat to Spain.

Leicester, courageous, self-confident, and sanguine as ever; could not restrain his indignation at the parsimony with which his own impatient spirit had to contend. "Be you assured," said he, on the 3rd August, when the Armada was off the Isle of Wight, "if the Spanish fleet arrive safely in the narrow seas, the Duke of Parma will join presently with all his forces, and lose no time in invading this realm. Therefore I beseech you, my good Lords, let no man, by hope or other abuse; prevent your speedy providing defence against, this mighty enemy now knocking at our gate."

For even at this supreme moment doubts were entertained at court as to the intentions of the Spaniards:

Next day he informed Walsingham that his four thousand men had arrived. "They be as forward men and willing to meet the enemy as I ever saw," said he. He could not say as much in, praise of the commissariat: "Some want the captains showed," he observed, "for these men arrived without one meal of victuals so that on their-arrival, they had not one barrel of beer nor loaf of bread—enough after twenty miles' march to have discouraged them, and brought them to mutiny. I see many causes to increase my former opinion of the dilatory wants you shall find upon all sudden hurley burleys. In no former time was ever so great a cause, and albeit her Majesty hath appointed an army to resist her enemies if they land, yet how hard a matter it will be to gather men together, I find it now. If it will be five days to gather these countrymen, judge what it will be to look in short space for those that dwell forty, fifty, sixty miles off."

He had immense difficulty in feeding even this slender force. "I made proclamation," said he, "two days ago, in all market towns, that victuallers should come to the camp and receive money for their provisions, but there is not one victualler come in to this hour. I have sent to all the justices of peace about it from place to place. I speak it that timely consideration be had of these things, and that they be not deferred till the worst come. Let her Majesty not defer the time, upon any supposed hope, to assemble a convenient force of horse and foot about her. Her Majesty cannot be strong enough too soon, and if her navy had not been strong and abroad as it is, what care had herself and her whole realm been in by this time! And what care she will be in if her forces be not only assembled, but an army presently dressed to withstand the mighty enemy that is to approach her gates."

"God doth know, I speak it not to bring her to charges. I would she had less cause to spend than ever she had, and her coffers fuller than ever they were; but I will prefer her life and safety, and the defence of the realm, before all sparing of charges in the present danger."

Thus, on the 5th August, no army had been assembled—not even the body- guard of the Queen—and Leicester, with four thousand men, unprovided with a barrel of beer or a loaf of bread, was about commencing his entrenched camp at Tilbury. On the 6th August the Armada was in Calais roads, expecting Alexander Farnese to lead his troops upon London!

Norris and Williams, on the news of Medina Sidonia's approach, had rushed to Dover, much to the indignation of Leicester, just as the Earl was beginning his entrenchments at Tilbury. "I assure you I am angry with Sir John Norris and Sir Roger Williams," he said. "I am here cook, caterer, and huntsman. I am left with no one to supply Sir John's place as marshal, but, for a day or two, am willing to work the harder myself. I ordered them both to return this day early, which they faithfully promised. Yet, on arriving this morning, I hear nothing of either, and have nobody to marshal the camp either for horse or foot. This manner of dealing doth much mislike me in them both. I am ill-used. 'Tis now four o'clock, but here's not one of them. If they come not this night, I assure you I will not receive them into office, nor bear such loose careless dealing at their hands. If you saw how weakly I am assisted you would be sorry to think that we here, should be the front against the enemy that is so mighty, if he should land here. And seeing her Majesty hath appointed me her lieutenant-general, I look that respect be used towards me, such as is due to my place."

Thus the ancient grudge—between Leicester and the Earl of Sussex's son was ever breaking forth, and was not likely to prove beneficial at this eventful season.

Next day the Welshman arrived, and Sir John promised to come back in the evening. Sir Roger brought word from the coast that Lord Henry Seymour's fleet was in want both of men and powder. "Good Lord!" exclaimed Leicester, "how is this come to pass, that both he and, my Lord-Admiral are so weakened of men. I hear they be running away. I beseech you, assemble your forces, and play not away this kingdom by delays. Hasten our horsemen hither and footmen: . . . . If the Spanish fleet come to the narrow seas the, Prince of Parma will play another part than is looked for."

As the Armada approached Calais, Leicester was informed that the soldiers at Dover began to leave the coast. It seemed that they were dissatisfied with the penuriousness of the government. Our soldiers do break away at Dover, or are not pleased. I assure you, without wages, the people will not tarry, and contributions go hard with them. Surely I find that her Majesty must needs deal liberally, and be at charges to entertain her subjects that have chargeably, and liberally used, themselves to serve her." The lieutenant-general even thought it might be necessary for him to proceed to Dover in person, in order to remonstrate with these discontented troops; for it was possible that those ill-paid, undisciplined, and very meagre forces, would find much difficulty in opposing Alexander's march, to London, if he should once succeed in landing. Leicester had a very indifferent opinion too of the train-bands of the metropolis. "For your Londoners," he said, "I see their service will be little, except they have their own captains, and having them, I look for none at all by them, when we shall meet the enemy. This was not complimentary, certainly, to the training of the famous Artillery Garden, and furnished a still stronger motive for defending the road over which the capital was to be approached. But there was much jealousy, both among citizens and nobles, of any authority entrusted to professional soldiers. "I know what burghers be, well enough," said the Earl, "as brave and well-entertained as ever the Londoners were. If they should go forth from the city they should have good leaders. You know the imperfections of the time, how few-leaders you have, and the gentlemen of the counties are very loth to have any captains placed with them. So that the beating out of our best captains is like to be cause of great danger."'

Sir John Smith, a soldier of experience, employed to drill and organize some of the levies, expressed still more disparaging opinions than those of Leicester concerning the probable efficiency in the field of these English armies. The Earl was very angry with the knight, however, and considered, him incompetent, insolent, and ridiculous. Sir John seemed, indeed, more disposed to keep himself out of harm's way, than to render service to the Queen by leading awkward recruits against Alexander Farnese. He thought it better to nurse himself.

"You would laugh to see how Sir John Smith has dealt since my coming," said Leicester. "He came to me, and told me that his disease so grew upon him as he must needs go to the baths. I told him I would not be against his health, but he saw what the time was, and what pains he had taken with his countrymen, and that I had provided a good place for him. Next day he came again, saying little to my offer then, and seemed desirous, for his health, to be gone. I told him what place I did appoint, which was a regiment of a great part of his countrymen. He said his health was dear to him, and he desired to take leave of me, which I yielded unto. Yesterday, being our muster-day, he came again to me to dinner; but such foolish and vain-glorious paradoxes he burst withal, without any cause offered, as made all that knew anything smile and answer little, but in sort rather to satisfy men present than to argue with him."

And the knight went that day to review Leicester's choice troops—the four thousand men of Essex—but was not much more deeply impressed with their proficiency than he had been with that of his own regiment. He became very censorious.

"After the muster," said the lieutenant-general, "he entered again into such strange cries for ordering of men, and for the fight with the weapon, as made me think he was not well. God forbid he should have charge of men that knoweth so little, as I dare pronounce that he doth."

Yet the critical knight was a professional—campaigner, whose opinions were entitled to respect; and the more so, it would seem, because they did not materially vary from those which Leicester himself was in the habit of expressing. And these interior scenes of discord, tumult, parsimony, want of organization, and unsatisfactory mustering of troops, were occurring on the very Saturday and Sunday when the Armada lay in sight of Dover cliffs, and when the approach of the Spaniards on the Dover road might at any moment be expected.

Leicester's jealous and overbearing temper itself was also proving a formidable obstacle to a wholesome system of defence. He was already displeased with the amount of authority entrusted to Lord Hunsdon, disposed to think his own rights invaded; and desirous that the Lord Chamberlain should accept office under himself. He wished saving clauses as to his own authority inserted in Hunsdon's patent. "Either it must be so, or I shall have wrong," said he, "if he absolutely command where my patent doth give me power. You may easily conceive what absurd dealings are likely to fall out, if you allow two absolute commanders."

Looking at these pictures of commander-in-chief, officers, and rank and file—as painted by themselves—we feel an inexpressible satisfaction that in this great crisis of England's destiny, there were such men as Howard, Drake, Frobisher, Hawkins, Seymour, Winter, Fenner, and their gallant brethren, cruising that week in the Channel, and that Nassau and Warmond; De Moor and Van der Does, were blockading the Flemish coast.

There was but little preparation to resist the enemy once landed. There were no fortresses, no regular army, no population trained to any weapon. There were patriotism, loyalty, courage, and enthusiasm, in abundance; but the commander-in-chief was a queen's favourite, odious to the people, with very moderate abilities, and eternally quarrelling with officers more competent than himself; and all the arrangements were so hopelessly behind-hand, that although great disasters might have been avenged, they could scarcely have been avoided.

Remembering that the Invincible Armada was lying in Calais roads on the 6th of August, hoping to cross to Dover the next morning, let us ponder the words addressed on that very day to Queen Elizabeth by the Lieutenant-General of England.

"My most dear and gracious Lady," said the Earl, "it is most true that those enemies that approach your kingdom and person are your undeserved foes, and being so, and hating you for a righteous cause, there is the less fear to be had of their malice or their forces; for there is a most just God that beholdeth the innocence of that heart. The cause you are assailed for is His and His Church's, and He never failed any that faithfully do put their chief trust in His goodness. He hath, to comfort you withal, given you great and mighty means to defend yourself, which means I doubt not but your Majesty will timely and princely use them, and your good God that ruleth all will assist you and bless you with victory."

He then proceeded to give his opinion on two points concerning which the Queen had just consulted him—the propriety of assembling her army, and her desire to place herself at the head of it in person.

On the first point one would have thought discussion superfluous on the 6th of August. "For your army, it is more than time it were gathered and about you," said Leicester, "or so near you as you may have the use of it at a few hours' warning. The reason is that your mighty enemies are at hand, and if God suffers them to pass by your fleet, you are sure they will attempt their purpose of landing with all expedition. And albeit your navy be very strong, but, as we have always heard, the other is not only far greater, but their forces of men much beyond yours. No doubt if the Prince of Parma come forth, their forces by sea shall not only be greatly, augmented, but his power to land shall the easier take effect whensoever he shall attempt it. Therefore it is most requisite that your Majesty at all events have as great a force every way as you can devise; for there is no dalliance at such a time, nor with such an enemy. You shall otherwise hazard your own honour, besides your person and country, and must offend your gracious God that gave you these forces and power, though you will not use them when you should."

It seems strange enough that such phrases should be necessary when the enemy was knocking at the gate; but it is only too, true that the land- forces were never organized until the hour, of danger had, most fortunately and unexpectedly, passed by. Suggestions at this late moment were now given for the defence of the throne, the capital, the kingdom, and the life of the great Queen, which would not have seemed premature had they been made six months before, but which, when offered in August, excite unbounded amazement.

Alexander would have had time to, march from Dover to Duxham before these directions, now leisurely stated with all the air of novelty, could be carried into effect.

"Now for the placing of your army," says the lieutenant-general on the memorable Saturday, 6th of August, "no doubt but I think about London the, meetest, and I suppose that others will be of the same mind. And your Majesty should forthwith give the charge thereof to some special nobleman about you, and likewise place all your chief officers that every man may know what he shall do, and gather as many good horse above all things as you can, and the oldest, best, and assuredest captains to lead; for therein will consist the greatest hope of good success under God. And so soon as your army is assembled, let them by and by be exercised, every man to know his weapon, and that there be all other things prepared in readiness, for your army, as if they should march upon a day's warning, especially carriages, and a commissary of victuals, and a master of ordnance."

Certainly, with Alexander of Parma on his way to London, at the head of his Italian pikemen, his Spanish musketeers, his famous veteran legion— "that nursing mother of great soldiers"—it was indeed more than time. that every man should know what he should do, that an army of Englishmen should be-assembled, and that every man should know his weapon. "By and by" was easily said, and yet, on the 6th of August it was by and by that an army, not yet mustered, not yet officered, not yet provided with a general, a commissary of victuals, or a master of ordinance, was to be exercised, "every man to know his weapon."

English courage might ultimately triumph over, the mistakes of those who governed the country, and over those disciplined brigands by whom it was to be invaded. But meantime every man of those invaders had already learned on a hundred battle-fields to know his weapon.

It was a magnificent determination on the part of Elizabeth to place herself at the head of her troops; and the enthusiasm which her attitude inspired, when she had at last emancipated herself from the delusions of diplomacy and the seductions of thrift, was some recompense at least for the perils caused by her procrastination. But

Leicester could not approve of this hazardous though heroic resolution.

The danger passed away. The Invincible Armada was driven out of the Channel by the courage; the splendid seamanship, and the enthusiasm of English sailors and volunteers. The Duke of Parma was kept a close prisoner by the fleets of Holland and Zeeland; and the great storm of the 14th and 15th of August at last completed the overthrow of the Spaniards.

It was, however, supposed for a long time that they would come back, for the disasters which had befallen them in the north were but tardily known in England. The sailors, by whom England had been thus defended in her utmost need, were dying by hundreds, and even thousands, of ship-fever, in the latter days of August. Men sickened one day, and died the next, so that it seemed probable that the ten thousand sailors by whom the English ships of war were manned, would have almost wholly disappeared, at a moment when their services might be imperatively required. Nor had there been the least precaution taken for cherishing and saving these brave defenders of their country. They rotted in their ships, or died in the streets of the naval ports, because there were no hospitals to receive them.

"'Tis a most pitiful sight," said the Lord-Admiral, "to see here at Margate how the men, having no place where they can be received, die in, the streets. I am driven of force myself to come on land to see them bestowed in some lodgings; and the best I can get is barns and such outhouses, and the relief is small that I can provide for them here. It would grieve any man's heart to see men that have served so valiantly die so miserably."

The survivors, too, were greatly discontented; for, after having been eight months at sea, and enduring great privations, they could not get their wages. "Finding it to come thus scantily," said Howard, "it breeds a marvellous alteration among them."

But more dangerous than the pestilence or the discontent was the misunderstanding which existed at the moment between the leading admirals of the English fleet. Not only was Seymour angry with Howard, but Hawkins and Frobisher were at daggers drawn with Drake; and Sir Martin— if contemporary, affidavits can be trusted—

did not scruple to heap the most virulent abuse upon Sir Francis, calling him, in language better fitted for the forecastle than the quarter-deck, a thief and a coward, for appropriating the ransom for Don Pedro Valdez in which both Frobisher and Hawkins claimed at least an equal share with himself.

And anxious enough was the Lord-Admiral with his sailors perishing by pestilence, with many of his ships so weakly manned that as Lord Henry Seymour declared there were not mariners enough to weigh the anchors, and with the great naval heroes, on whose efforts the safety of the realm depended, wrangling like fisherwomen among themselves, when rumours came, as they did almost daily, of the return of the Spanish Armada, and of new demonstrations on the part of Farnese. He was naturally unwilling that the fruits of English valour on the seas should now be sacrificed by the false economy of the government. He felt that, after all that had been endured and accomplished, the Queen and her counsellors were still capable of leaving England at the mercy of a renewed attempt, "I know not what you think at the court," said he; "but I think, and so do all here, that there cannot be too great forces maintained for the next five or six weeks. God knoweth whether the Spanish fleet will not, after refreshing themselves in Norway; Denmark, and the Orkneys, return. I think they dare not go back to Sprain with this, dishonour, to their King and overthrow of the Pope's credit. Sir, sure bind, sure find. A kingdom is a grand wager. Security is dangerous; and, if God had not been our best friend; we should have found it so."

[Howard to Walsingham, Aug.8/18 1588. (S. P. Office MS.)]

> ["Some haply may say that winter cometh on apace," said Drake, "but my poor opinion is that I dare not advise her Majesty to hazard a kingdom with the saving of a little charge." (Drake to Walsingham, Aug. 8/18 1588.)]

Nothing could be more replete, with sound common sense than this simple advice, given as it was in utter ignorance of the fate of the Armada; after it had been lost sight of by the English vessels off the Firth of Forth, and of the cold refreshment which: it had found in Norway and the Orkneys. But, Burghley had a store of pithy apophthegms, for which—he knew he could always find sympathy in the Queen's breast, and with which he could answer these demands of admirals and generals. "To spend in time convenient is wisdom;" he observed—"to continue charges without needful cause bringeth, repentance;"—"to hold on charges without knowledge of the certainty thereof and of means how to support them, is lack of wisdom;" and so on.

Yet the Spanish fleet might have returned into the Channel for ought the Lord-Treasurer on the 22nd August knew—or the Dutch fleet might have relaxed, in its vigilant watching of Farnese's movements. It might have then seemed a most plentiful lack of wisdom to allow English sailors to die of plague in the streets for want of hospitals; and to grow mutinous for default of pay. To have saved under such circumstances would, perhaps have brought repentance.

The invasion of England by Spain had been most portentous. That the danger was at last averted is to be ascribed to the enthusiasm of the English, nation—both patricians and plebeians—to the heroism of the little English fleet, to the spirit of the naval commanders and volunteers, to the stanch, and effective support of the Hollanders; and to the hand of God shattering the Armada at last; but very little credit can be conscientiously awarded to the diplomatic or the military efforts of the Queen's government. Miracles alone, in the opinion of Roger Williams, had saved England on this occasion from perdition.

Towards the end of August, Admiral de Nassau paid a visit to Dover with forty ships, "well appointed and furnished." He dined and conferred with Seymour, Palmer, and other officers—Winter being still laid up with his wound—and expressed the opinion that Medina Sidonia would hardly return to the Channel, after the banquet he had received from her Majesty's navy between Calais and Gravelines. He also gave the information that the States had sent fifty Dutch vessels in pursuit of the Spaniards, and had compelled all the herring-fishermen for the time to serve in the ships of war, although the prosperity of the country depended on that industry. "I find the man very wise, subtle, and cunning," said Seymour of the Dutch Admiral, "and therefore do I trust him."

Nassau represented the Duke of Parma as evidently discouraged, as having already disembarked his troops, and as very little disposed to hazard any further enterprise against England. "I have left twenty-five Kromstevens," said he, "to prevent his egress from Sluys, and I am immediately returning thither myself. The tide will not allow his vessels at present to leave Dunkerk, and I shall not fail—before the next full moon—to place myself before that place, to prevent their coming out, or to have a brush with them if they venture to put to sea."

But after the scenes on which the last full moon had looked down in those waters, there could be no further pretence on the part of Farnese to issue from Sluys and Dunkerk, and England and Holland were thenceforth saved from all naval enterprises on the part of Spain.

Meantime, the same uncertainty which prevailed in England as to the condition and the intentions of the Armada was still more remarkable elsewhere. There was a systematic deception practised not only upon other governments; but upon the King of Spain as well. Philip, as he sat at his writing-desk, was regarding himself as the monarch of England, long after his Armada had been hopelessly dispersed.

In Paris, rumours were circulated during the first ten days of August that England was vanquished, and that the Queen was already on her way to Rome as a prisoner, where she was to make expiation, barefoot, before his Holiness. Mendoza, now more magnificent than ever—stalked into Notre Dame with his drawn sword in his hand, crying out with a loud voice, "Victory, victory!" and on the 10th of August ordered bonfires to be made before his house; but afterwards thought better of that scheme. He had been deceived by a variety of reports sent to him day after day by agents on the coast; and the King of France—better informed by Stafford, but not unwilling thus to feed his spite against the insolent ambassador—affected to believe his fables. He even confirmed them by intelligence, which he pretended to have himself received from other sources, of the landing of the Spaniards in England without opposition, and of the entire subjugation of that country without the striking of a blow.

Hereupon, on the night of August 10th, the envoy—"like a wise man," as Stafford observed—sent off four couriers, one after another, with the great news to Spain, that his master's heart might be rejoiced, and caused a pamphlet on the subject to be printed and distributed over Paris! "I will not waste a large sheet of paper to express the joy which we must all feel," he wrote to Idiaquez, "at this good news. God be praised for all, who gives us small chastisements to make us better, and then, like a merciful Father, sends us infinite rewards." And in the same strain he wrote; day after day, to Moura and Idiaquez, and to Philip himself.

Stafford, on his side, was anxious to be informed by his government of the exact truth, whatever it were, in order that these figments of Mendoza might be contradicted. "That which cometh from me," he said, "Will be believed; for I have not been used to tell lies, and in very truth I have not the face to do it."

And the news of the Calais squibs, of the fight off Gravelines, and the retreat of the Armada towards the north; could not be very long concealed. So soon, therefore, as authentic intelligence reached, the English envoy of those events—which was not however for nearly ten days after their—occurrence—Stafford in his turn wrote a pamphlet, in answer to that of Mendoza, and decidedly the more successful one of the two. It cost him but five crowns, he said, to print 'four hundred copies of it; but those in whose name it was published got one hundred crowns by its sale. The English ambassador was unwilling to be known as the author—although "desirous of touching up the impudence of the Spaniard" —but the King had no doubt of its origin. Poor Henry, still smarting under the insults of Mendoza and 'Mucio,—was delighted with this blow to Philip's presumption; was loud in his praises of Queen Elizabeth's valour, prudence, and marvellous fortune, and declared that what she had just done could be compared to the greatest: exploits of the most illustrious men in history.

"So soon as ever he saw the pamphlet," said Stafford; "he offered to lay a wager it was my doing; and laughed at it heartily." And there were malicious pages about the French; court; who also found much amusement in writing to the ambassador, begging his interest with the Duke of Parma that they might obtain from that conqueror some odd-refuse town or so in: England, such as York, Canterbury, London, or the like—till the luckless Don Bernardino was ashamed to show his face.

A letter, from Farnese, however, of 10th August, apprized Philip before the end of August of the Calais disasters and caused him great uneasiness, without driving him to despair. "At the very moment," wrote the King to Medina Sidonia; "when I was expecting news of the effect hoped for from my Armada, I have learned the retreat from before Calais, to which it was compelled by the weather; [!] and I have received a very great shock which keeps, me in anxiety not to be exaggerated. Nevertheless I hope in our Lord that he will have provided a remedy; and that if it was possible for you to return upon the enemy to come back to the appointed posts and to watch an opportunity for the great stroke; you will have done as the case required; and so I am expecting with solicitude, to hear what has happened, and please God it may be that which is so suitable for his service."

His Spanish children the sacking of London, and the butchering of the English nation rewards and befits similar to those which they bad formerly enjoyed in the Netherlands.

And in the same strain, melancholy yet hopeful, were other letters despatched on that day to the Duke of Parma. "The satisfaction caused by your advices on the 8th August of the arrival of the Armada near Calais, and of your preparations to embark your troops, was changed into a sentiment which you can imagine, by your letter of the 10th. The anxiety thus occasioned it would be impossible to exaggerate, although the cause being such as it is—there is no ground for distrust. Perhaps the Armada, keeping together, has returned upon the enemy, and given a good account of itself, with the help of the Lord. So I still promise myself that you will have performed your part in the enterprise in such wise as that the service intended to the Lord may have been executed, and repairs made to the reputation of all; which has been so much compromised."

And the King's drooping spirits were revived by fresh accounts which reached him in September, by way of France. He now learned that the Armada had taken captive four Dutch men-of-war and many English ships; that, after the Spaniards had been followed from Calais roads by the enemy's fleet, there had been an action, which the English had attempted in vain to avoid; off Newcastle; that Medina Sidonia had charged upon them so vigorously, as to sink twenty of their ships, and to capture twenty-six others, good and sound; that the others, to escape perdition, had fled, after suffering great damage, and had then gone to pieces, all hands perishing; that the Armada had taken a port in Scotland, where it was very comfortably established; that the flag-ship of Lord-admiral Howard, of Drake; and of that "distinguished mariner Hawkins," had all been sunk in action, and that no soul had been saved except Drake, who had escaped in a cock-boat. "This is good news," added the writer; "and it is most certain."

The King pondered seriously over these conflicting accounts, and remained very much in the dark. Half, the month of September went by, and he had heard nothing—official since the news of the Calais catastrophe. It may be easily understood that Medina Sidonia, while flying round the Orkneys had not much opportunity for despatching couriers to Spain, and as Farnese had not written since the 10th August, Philip was quite at a loss whether to consider himself triumphant or defeated. From the reports by way of Calais, Dunkerk, and Rouen, he supposed that the Armada, had inflicted much damage on the enemy. He suggested accordingly, on the 3rd September, to the Duke of Parma, that he might now make the passage to England, while the English fleet, if anything was left of it was repairing its damages. "'Twill be easy enough to conquer the country," said Philip," so soon as you set foot on the soil. Then perhaps our Armada can come back and station itself in the Thames to support you."

Nothing could be simpler. Nevertheless the King felt a pang of doubt lest affairs, after all, might not be going on so swimmingly; so he dipped his pen in the inkstand again, and observed with much pathos, "But if this hope must be given up, you must take the Isle of Walcheren: something must be done to console me."

And on the 15th September he was still no wiser. "This business of the Armada leaves me no repose," he said; "I can think of nothing else. I don't content myself with what I have written, but write again and again, although in great want of light. I hear that the Armada has sunk and captured many English ships, and is refitting in a Scotch pert. If this is in the territory, of Lord Huntley, I hope he will stir up the Catholics of that country."

And so, in letter after letter, Philip clung to the delusion that Alexander could yet, cross to England, and that the Armada might sail up the Thames. The Duke was directed to make immediate arrangements to that effect with Medina Sidonia, at the very moment when that tempest-tossed grandee was painfully-creeping back towards the Bay of Biscay, with what remained of his invincible fleet.

Sanguine and pertinacious, the King refused to believe in, the downfall of his long-cherished scheme; and even when the light was at last dawning upon him, he was like a child, crying for a fresh toy, when the one which had long amused him had been broken. If the Armada were really very much damaged, it was easy enough, he thought, for the Duke of Parma to make him a new one, while the old, one was repairing. "In case the Armada is too much shattered to come out," said Philip, "and winter compels it to stay in that port, you must cause another Armada to be constructed at Emden and the adjacent towns, at my expense, and, with the two together, you will certainly be able to conquer England."

And he wrote to Medina Sidonia in similar terms. That naval commander was instructed to enter the Thames at once, if strong enough. If not, he was to winter in the Scotch port which he was supposed to have captured. Meantime Farnese would build a new fleet at Emden, and in the spring the two dukes would proceed to accomplish the great purpose.

But at last the arrival of Medina Sidonia at Santander dispelled these visions, and now the King appeared in another attitude. A messenger, coming post-haste from the captain-general, arrived in the early days of October at the Escorial. Entering the palace he found Idiaquez and Moura pacing up and down the corridor, before the door of Philip's cabinet, and was immediately interrogated by those counsellors, most anxious, of course, to receive authentic intelligence at last as to the fate, of the Armada. The entire overthrow of the great project was now, for the first time, fully revealed in Spain;

the fabulous victories over the English, and the annihilation of Howard and all his ships, were dispersed in air. Broken, ruined, forlorn, the invincible Armada—so far as it still existed—had reached a Spanish port. Great was the consternation of Idiaquez and Moura, as they listened to the tale, and very desirous was each of the two secretaries that the other should, discharge the unwelcome duty of communicating the fatal intelligence to the King.

At last Moura consented to undertake the task, and entering the cabinet, he found Philip seated at his desk. Of course he was writing letters. Being informed of the arrival of a messenger from the north, he laid down his pen, and inquired the news. The secretary replied that the accounts, concerning the Armada were by no means so favourable as, could be wished. The courier was then introduced, and made his dismal report. The King did not change countenance. "Great thanks," he observed, "do I render to Almighty God, by whose generous hand I am gifted with such power, that I could easily, if I chose, place another fleet upon the seas. Nor is it of very great importance that a running stream should be sometimes intercepted, so long as the fountain from which it flows remains inexhaustible."

So saying he resumed his pen, and serenely proceeded with his letters. Christopher Moura stared with unaffected amazement at his sovereign, thus tranquil while a shattered world was falling on his head, and then retired to confer with his colleague.

"And how did his Majesty receive the blow?" asked Idiaquez.

"His Majesty thinks nothing of the blow," answered Moura, "nor do I, consequently, make more of this great calamity than does his Majesty."

So the King—as fortune flew away from him, wrapped himself in his virtue; and his counsellors, imitating their sovereign, arrayed themselves in the same garment. Thus draped, they were all prepared to bide the pelting of the storm which was only beating figuratively on their heads, while it had been dashing the King's mighty galleons on the rocks, and drowning by thousands the wretched victims of his ambition. Soon afterwards, when the particulars of the great disaster were thoroughly known, Philip ordered a letter to be addressed in his name to all the bishops of Spain, ordering a solemn thanksgiving to the Almighty for the safety of that portion of the invincible Armada which it had pleased Him to preserve.

And thus, with the sound of mourning throughout Spain—for there was scarce a household of which some beloved member had not perished in the great catastrophe—and with the peals of merry bells over all England and Holland, and with a solemn 'Te Deum' resounding in every church, the curtain fell upon the great tragedy of the Armada.